#BESTIE

# Bestie

BESTIE

An Hachette UK Company
www.hachette.co.uk

Summersdale Publishers Ltd
Part of Octopus Publishing Group Limited
Carmelite House
50 Victoria Embankment
LONDON
EC4Y 0DZ
UK

www.summersdale.com

Printed and bound in Poland

ISBN: 978-1-83799-399-4

Substantial discounts on bulk quantities of Summersdale books are available to corporations, professional associations and other organizations. For details contact general enquiries: telephone: +44 (0) 1243 771107 or email: enquiries@summersdale.com.

# Bestie

summersdale

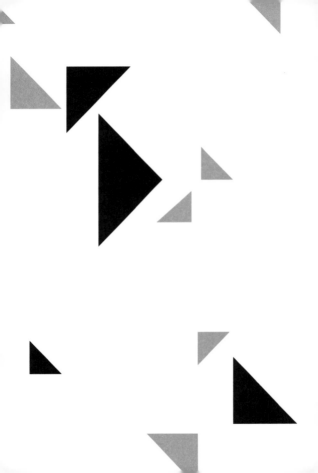

To......................................

From.................................

# DEAR BESTIE, I HONESTLY DON'T KNOW

# WHAT I'D DO WITHOUT YOU

**True friends are like diamonds — bright, beautiful, valuable and always in style.**

Nicole Richie

# Women are the largest untapped reservoir of talent in the world.

Hillary Clinton

# Some girls are just born with glitter in their veins

# NO ONE CAN MAKE YOU FEEL INFERIOR WITHOUT YOUR CONSENT.

Eleanor Roosevelt

**Never give up, for that is just the place and time that the tide will turn.**

Harriet Beecher Stowe

If a woman is sufficiently ambitious, determined and gifted – there is practically nothing she can't do.

Helen Lawrenson

**ONE GIRL CAN MAKE A DIFFERENCE**

**TWO GIRLS CAN CHANGE THE WORLD**

# = BEST
# FRIEND
# GOALS

I like you
because we hate
the same stuff

# ONE IS NOT BORN, BUT RATHER BECOMES, A WOMAN.

Simone de Beauvoir

**You only live once, but if you do it right, once is enough.**

Mae West

You grow up the day
you have the first real
laugh at yourself.

Ethel Barrymore

#Babe

A LOT OF PEOPLE ARE AFRAID TO SAY WHAT THEY WANT. THAT'S WHY THEY DON'T GET WHAT THEY WANT.

Madonna

**SHE'S BRIGHT LIKE GLITTER AND BUBBLY LIKE CHAMPAGNE...**

# AND SHARP
# LIKE BARBED
# WIRE

# Wherever we are, it is our friends that make our world.

Henry Drummond

I think that sometimes being fearless is having fears but jumping anyway.

**Taylor Swift**

**Everything in my life, every answer in my life, every opportunity is always my decision.**

Nicki Minaj

# In my moments of doubt I've told myself firmly – if not me, who? If not now, when?

Emma Watson

# We're not afraid to sparkle

A FRIEND IS ONE
THAT KNOWS
YOU AS YOU
ARE, ACCEPTS
WHAT YOU HAVE
BECOME AND
ALLOWS YOU
TO GROW.

Anonymous

# Nothing is better than a friend, unless it is a friend with chocolate.

Linda Grayson

Girl squad

# PRINCESS?

# NO, LADY: QUEEN

A girl doesn't need
anyone who doesn't
need her.

Marilyn Monroe

# WHEN A WOMAN BECOMES HER OWN BEST FRIEND
## LIFE IS EASIER.

Diane von Fürstenberg

# Believe in your inner Beyoncé

**Some souls just understand each other upon meeting.**

N. R. Hart

A true friend is someone who lets you have total freedom to be yourself.

Jim Morrison

# YOU CAN'T DO IT ALONE... OTHER PEOPLE AND OTHER PEOPLE'S IDEAS ARE OFTEN BETTER THAN YOUR OWN.

Amy Poehler

# I HOPE WE'RE FRIENDS UNTIL WE DIE...

THEN I HOPE
WE STAY
GHOST
FRIENDS
AND WALK
THROUGH
WALLS
SCARING THE
HELL OUT OF
PEOPLE

I embrace
mistakes. They
make you
who you are.

Beyoncé

# If you really want to fly, harness your power to your passion.

**Oprah Winfrey**

I'm not interested
in money, I just want
to be wonderful.

Marilyn Monroe

You are
awesome

# Be strong, love and believe in yourself.

Emma Watson

# DON'T GET BITTER, JUST GET BETTER.

Alyssa Edwards

#winning

If you obey
all the rules,
you miss all
the fun.

Katharine Hepburn

# 1 PLANET,
# 7 CONTINENTS,
# HUNDREDS OF
# COUNTRIES...

**AND I HAD THE
PRIVILEGE OF
MEETING YOU**

A woman is like a teabag
– you can't tell how
strong she is until she
gets into hot water.

Anonymous

# IGNORE
## THE HATERS

**The most courageous act is still to think for yourself. Aloud.**

Coco Chanel

Dream crazy big

**My best friend is
the one who brings
out the best in me.**

Henry Ford

# THERE ARE TWO WAYS OF SPREADING LIGHT: TO BE THE CANDLE OR THE MIRROR THAT REFLECTS IT.

Edith Wharton

# YOU ONLY
# LIVE ONCE,

# SO YOU MIGHT AS WELL SLAY!

Only your
real friends will
tell you when your
face is dirty.

Sicilian proverb

# Chin up –
# we've got this

The most
beautiful discovery
true friends make
is that they can grow
separately without
growing apart.

Elisabeth Foley

**Best friends
are hard to
find because
the very best is
already mine!**

**I think women are foolish to pretend they are equal to men, they are far superior and always have been.**

William Golding

# THE IMPORTANT THING IS NOT WHAT THEY THINK OF ME, BUT WHAT I THINK OF THEM.

Queen Victoria

# A girl should be two things: who and what she wants.

**Coco Chanel**

I don't want
other people to
decide who I am.
I want to decide
that for myself.

Emma Watson

# THANK YOU
# FOR BEING

# MY
# UNBIOLOGICAL
# SISTER

Own who
you are

# IT'S EASIER
# TO BE BRAVE
# WHEN YOU'RE
# NOT ALONE.

Amy Poehler

# Soul sister

No one has
ever been able to
tell me I couldn't do
something because
I was a girl.

Anne Hathaway

**Happiness and confidence are the prettiest things you can wear.**

Taylor Swift

# NO ONE WILL EVER BE AS ENTERTAINED BY US AS US

# OUR LAUGHS? LIMITLESS

# OUR MEMORIES? COUNTLESS

# OUR FRIENDSHIP? THE BEST!

# Doubt is a killer. You just have to know who you are and what you stand for.

Jennifer Lopez

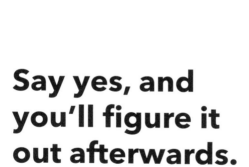

# Say yes, and you'll figure it out afterwards.

**Tina Fey**

**True friendship comes when silence between two people is comfortable.**

David Tyson Gentry

We can do
anything and
nothing,
and still have
the best time

# The love that comes with friendship is the underlying facet of a happy life.

Chelsea Handler

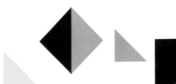

WE R 2 FAB

4 YOU

Don't be like anyone else. Find your voice, your script, your rhythms.

Jill Soloway

It's the friends
you can call up
at 4 a.m.
that matter.

Marlene Dietrich

# I THOUGHT
# I WAS
# NORMAL....

**UNTIL I MET
MY BEST
FRIEND**

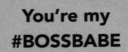

IT IS NOT SO
MUCH OUR
FRIENDS' HELP
THAT HELPS US
**AS THE
CONFIDENT
KNOWLEDGE
THAT THEY
WILL HELP US.**

Epicurus

**Too glam
to give
a damn**

You have what it takes
to be a victorious,
independent,
fearless woman.

Tyra Banks

**Always be a first-rate version of yourself, instead of a second-rate version of somebody else.**

Judy Garland

# IF YOU THINK YOU'RE TOO SMALL TO HAVE AN IMPACT, TRY GOING TO BED WITH A MOSQUITO.

Anita Roddick

# BOYS ARE WHATEVER,

**BEST FRIENDS
ARE FOREVER**

**Sassy
since birth**

# Girls should never be afraid to be smart.

**Emma Watson**

Don't waste your energy trying to educate or change opinions... Do your thing and don't care if they like it.

Tina Fey

You can't
be afraid of what
people are going
to say, because you're
never going to make
everyone happy.

Selena Gomez

I say if I'm beautiful.
I say if I'm strong.
You will not determine
my story – I will.

Amy Schumer

# NEVER DULL YOUR SHINE FOR SOMEBODY ELSE.

Tyra Banks

**Your vibe attracts your tribe**

# When someone tells you that you can't, turn around and say 'watch me'.

Anonymous

# SHE BELIEVED
# SHE COULD

**SO SHE DID**

A queen is not afraid to fail. Failure is another stepping stone to greatness.

Oprah Winfrey

IF YOU FALL,
I WILL ALWAYS
BE THERE TO
PICK YOU
UP... AFTER
I'VE FINISHED
LAUGHING!

**The question isn't who is going to let me, it's who is going to stop me.**

Ayn Rand

We call upon our sisters
around the world to
be brave — to embrace
the strength within
themselves and realise
their full potential.

Malala Yousafzai

**Don't you ever let a soul in the world tell you that you can't be exactly who you are.**

Lady Gaga

# I AM NOT AFRAID; I WAS BORN TO DO THIS.

Joan of Arc

# WE'LL ALWAYS BE BEST FRIENDS

# BECAUSE YOU KNOW TOO MUCH

**Rare as is
true love,
true friendship
is rarer.**

Jean de La Fontaine

I figure, if a girl
wants to be a legend,
she should just go
ahead and be one.

Calamity Jane

# Above all,
# be the heroine
# of your life,
# not the victim.

Nora Ephron

**Women have been trained to speak softly and carry a lipstick. Those days are over.**

Bella Abzug

YOU KNOW HOW CRAZY I AM, BUT YOU'RE STILL HAPPY TO BE SEEN WITH ME IN PUBLIC

Nothing can dim
the light which
shines from
within.

**Maya Angelou**

**Keep your friends close. Buy your enemies something cool.**

Lena Dunham

# BEST FRIEND
# IS A PROMISE

**NOT A LABEL**

A best friend is
like a four-leaf clover:
hard to find, and
lucky to have.

Sarah Jessica Parker

# TRUE FRIENDS ARE THOSE WHO REALLY KNOW YOU BUT LOVE YOU ANYWAY.

Edna Buchanan

# The best mirror is a friend's eye.

Gaelic proverb

I'm a big believer
in accepting yourself
the way you are and
not really worrying
about it.

Jennifer Lawrence

I think about my best friendship... as like a great romance of my young life.

Lena Dunham

# I ONLY
# ROLL WITH
# GODDESSES

# GROW OLD GRACEFULLY? NO CHANCE...

**WE'LL BE
TEARING UP
THE NURSING
HOME
TOGETHER**

Don't be
afraid to speak
up for yourself.
Keep fighting for
your dreams!

Gabby Douglas

I don't care what is written about me so long as it isn't true.

**Dorothy Parker**

Love you, bestie

# Attitude is everything.

Diane von Fürstenberg

**Female friendships that work are relationships in which women help each other belong to themselves.**

Louise Bernikow

# PARTNERS
# IN CRIME

You're only
young once,
but you can
be immature
forever.

**Germaine Greer**

You're pretty much my favourite person in the history of the world... ever

# KEEP CALM

**AND LOVE
YOUR BFF**

Any day spent with you is my favourite day. So today is my new favourite day.

A. A. Milne

YAAAAAAAASSSS
SSSSSSSSSSSS
SSSSSSSS!

# Each friend represents a world in us.

Anaïs Nin

# True friendship resists time, distance and silence.

Isabel Allende

# Always remember you're unique, just like everyone else.

Alison Boulter

# IF YOU HAVEN'T LEARNED THE MEANING OF FRIENDSHIP, YOU REALLY HAVEN'T LEARNED ANYTHING.

Muhammad Ali

# YOU'RE
# THE BEST

# OF THE
# BESTIES!

#squadgoals

**Sometimes you just have to put on lip gloss and pretend to be psyched.**

**Mindy Kaling**

**Other women
who are killing it
should motivate
you, thrill you,
challenge you and
inspire you.**

Taylor Swift

**There's power in looking silly and not caring that you do.**

Amy Poehler

# Be cool,
# hunny bunny

# USE EACH INTERACTION TO BE THE BEST, MOST POWERFUL VERSION OF YOURSELF.

Marianne Williamson

**SURROUND YOURSELF WITH THE THINGS YOU LOVE...**